Watching the Weather

Wind

Elizabeth Miles

H www.heinemann.co.uk/library

To order:
☎ Phone 44 (0) 1865 888066
📄 Send a fax to 44 (0) 1865 314091
💻 Visit the Heinemann Bookshop at www.heinemann.co.uk/library to browse our catalogue and order online.

First published in Great Britain by Heinemann Library, Halley Court, Jordan Hill, Oxford OX2 8EJ, part of Harcourt Education.
Heinemann is a registered trademark of Harcourt Education Ltd.

Editorial: Nancy Dickmann and Daniel Cuttelli
Design: Richard Parker and Q2A Solutions
Illustrations: Jeff Edwards
Picture Research: Maria Joannou and Lynda Lines
Production: Camilla Smith

Originated by Ambassador Litho Ltd.
Printed and bound in China by South China Printing Company

ISBN 0 431 19037 2
09 08 07 06 05
10 9 8 7 6 5 4 3 2 1

British Library Cataloguing in Publication Data
Miles, Elizabeth
    Wind. – (Watching the weather)
    551.5'18

A full catalogue record for this book is available from the British Library.

Acknowledgements
The Publishers would like to thank the following for permission to reproduce photographs: Alamy p.7 (Neil Setchfield); Corbis pp. 9, 13, 14 (Jim Sugar), 22 (Jim Reed), 23, 24, 25 (Jim Reed), 26, 27; Getty Images pp.8 (PhotoDisc), 12(Taxi/D Sim); Panos p. 21 (Clive Shirley); PA Photos p. 17 (EPA); Photolibrary.com p. 15 (Warwick Kent); PhotoDisc p.5; Reuters pp. 18 (Sherwin Crasto), 19 (Fatih Saribas); Rex Features pp. 4 (IJO), 20 (EDPPICS /SFinlay); Tudor Photography pp. 10, 28, 29.

Cover photograph of palm trees blowing in a gale reproduced with permission of Getty Images/Taxi.

The Publishers would like to thank Daniel Ogden for his assistance in the preparation of this book.

Every effort has been made to contact copyright holders of any material reproduced in this book. Any omissions will be rectified in subsequent printings if notice is given to the Publishers.

The paper used to print this book comes from sustainable resources.

Contents

Words appearing in the text in bold, **like this**, are explained in the Glossary.

 Find out more about wind at
www.heinemannexplore.co.uk

What is wind?

Wind is moving air. Air is all around us. Outside on a windy day you can feel the air blowing against your face.

We cannot see the wind but we can feel it push against us.

Wind pushes things along. It blows clouds across the sky and sailing boats across the sea. Winds can be fast or slow. They can feel strong or gentle.

We use the wind to fly kites.

Why do winds blow?

Winds blow because the sun heats the earth. Then, the earth warms the air above. The warm air rises, which makes cool air rush in to take its place.

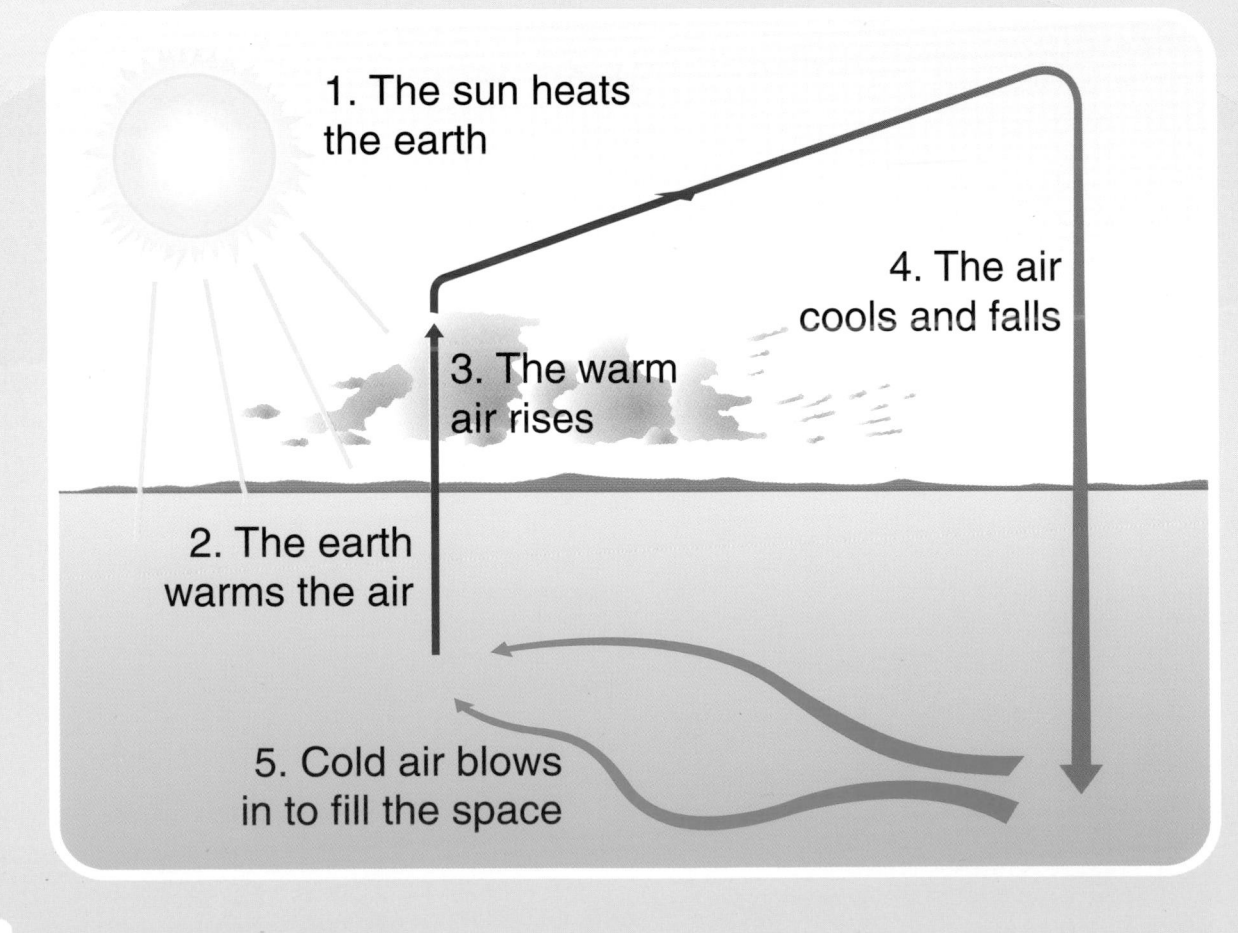

1. The sun heats the earth

4. The air cools and falls

3. The warm air rises

2. The earth warms the air

5. Cold air blows in to fill the space

A cool wind blowing in from the sea is sometimes called a sea **breeze**.

Some winds feel warm and some feel cool. When the land is warmer than the sea, cool winds can blow in from the sea.

Wind speed

Winds move at different speeds. Slower, gentler winds are called **breezes**. Faster, stronger winds are called **gales**. A gentle breeze blows only small or light things about.

Flags flutter in a gentle breeze.

A fast wind pushes a sailing boat along and can help it win a race.

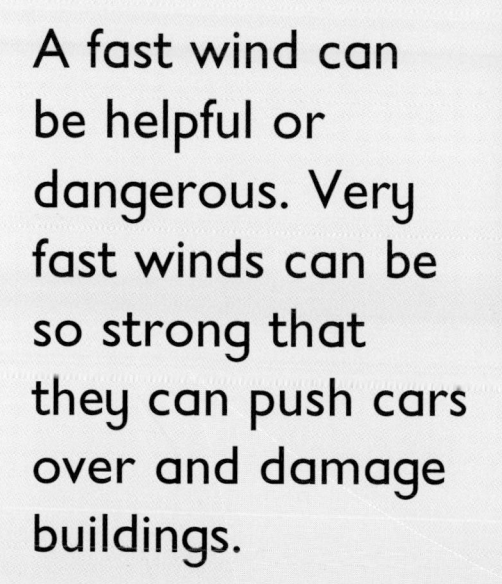

A fast wind can be helpful or dangerous. Very fast winds can be so strong that they can push cars over and damage buildings.

Measuring wind

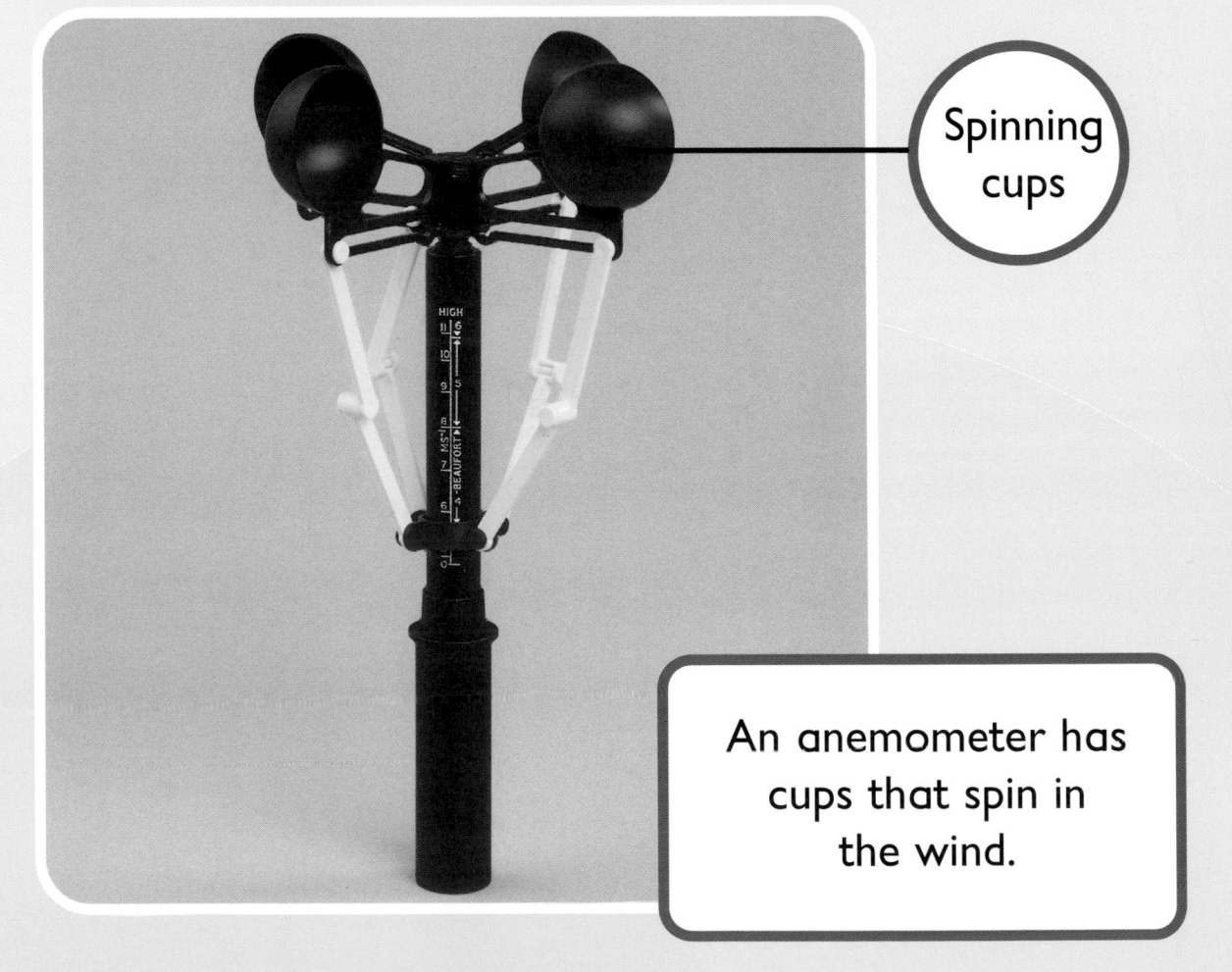

Spinning cups

An anemometer has cups that spin in the wind.

It is important to know the speed of a wind. The faster a wind, the more damage it can do. An **anemometer** is used to measure wind speed.

Francis Beaufort gave a list of names and numbers to winds of different strengths. It is called the Beaufort Scale. You can guess wind speeds by using it.

The Beaufort Scale			
Force	Speed	Description	Picture
1 Light air	1–5 km/h (1–3 mph)	Smoke shows the wind direction	
3 Gentle **breeze**	12–19 km/h (8–12 mph)	Loose paper blows around	
5 Fresh breeze	30–39 km/h (19–24 mph)	Leaves are blown off trees	
8 **Gale**	62–74 km/h (39–46 mph)	Twigs are broken from trees	
10 Storm	88–102 km/h (55–63 mph)	Trees are blown over	

Winds and storms

Powerful winds blow in a storm. During a storm, winds may blow down **power lines** and lift off the roofs of houses.

Strong winds at sea can make high waves.

A wind faster than 117 kilometres per hour (73 miles per hour) is called a hurricane.

The most dangerous storms are **hurricanes** and **tornadoes**. These bring winds that can pull up trees and blow down houses.

Wind direction

This **weather vane** shows the wind is blowing from the south.

Weather forecasters study wind direction to find out where the wind is blowing from. This helps them work out what sort of weather is coming.

People flying aircraft need to know the wind direction. Windsocks show the wind direction at airports. They point in the direction the wind is blowing.

Windsocks help people to fly aircraft safely.

Winds around the world

Some winds blow for short distances and last only a few hours. Other winds blow across longer distances and last for many weeks. We name winds after the direction they come from.

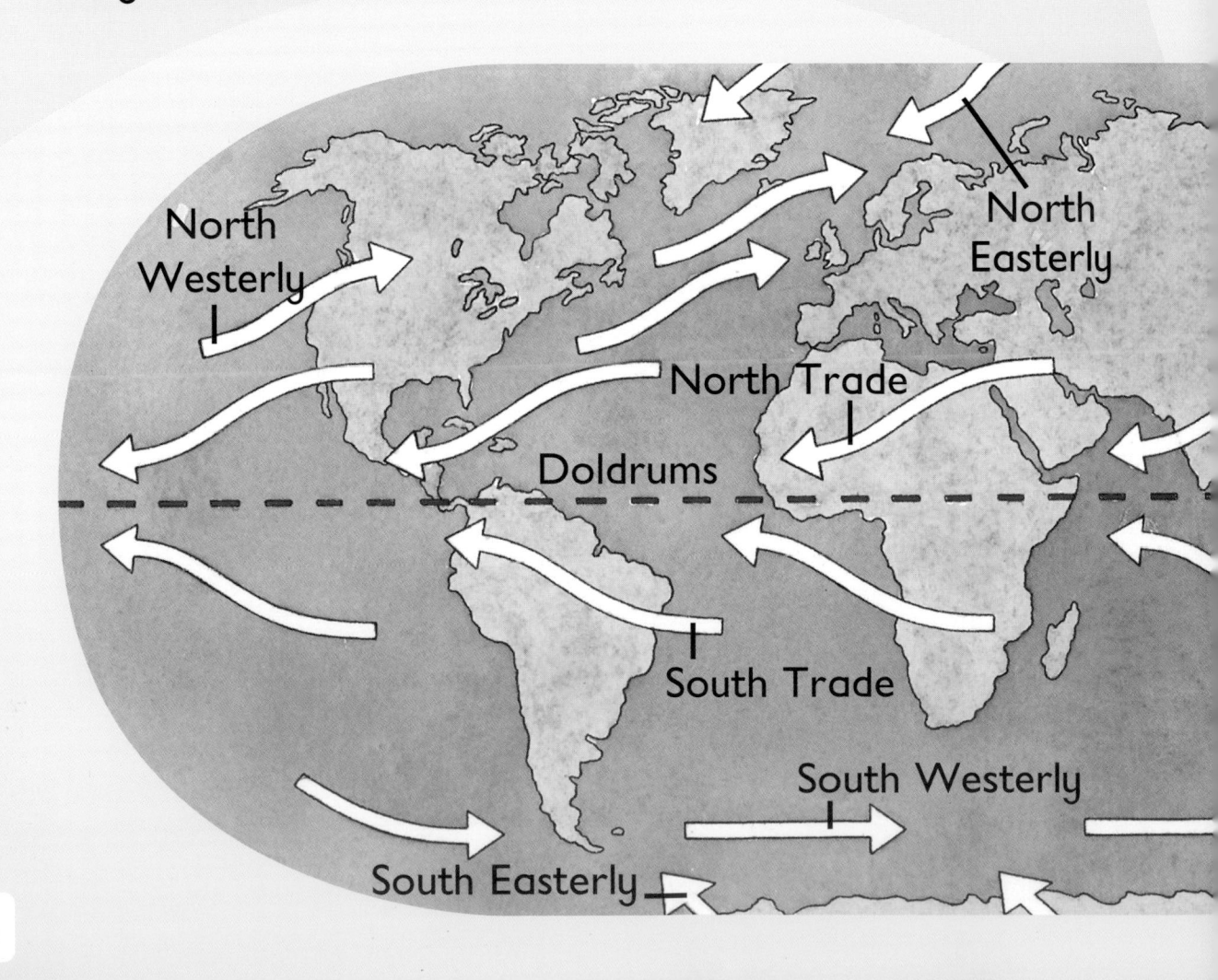

North Westerly

North Easterly

North Trade

Doldrums

South Trade

South Westerly

South Easterly

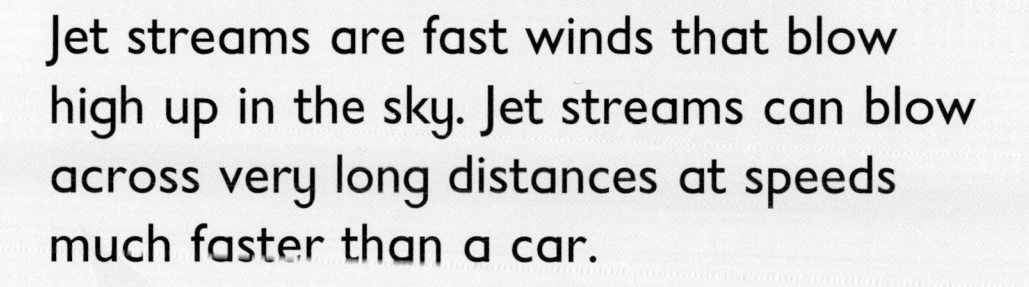

Jet stream winds can push aircraft and some hot air balloons along faster.

Jet streams are fast winds that blow high up in the sky. Jet streams can blow across very long distances at speeds much faster than a car.

Winds and the seasons

Different winds blow in different seasons.
In some places, **monsoon** winds blow in
summer. They bring lots of rain.

Monsoon winds can bring
lots of rain, which helps
crops grow.

Winter winds can bring icy weather to places where it is often warmer. The winds can bring freezing **temperatures** and snowstorms.

In winter, cold winds can cause snowstorms called blizzards.

Wind and plants

After a storm, blown-down trees may block roads. Sometimes they fall on houses.

Strong winds can damage **crops** and kill plants. They can even uproot trees and throw them across fields or roads.

Winds can blow soil away and kill plants. People put up **windbreaks** to stop the wind from damaging their plants.

A windbreak helps these people stop their land being turned into desert.

Wind and people

Winds can cause accidents. Powerful winds can push cars off the road or turn lorries over. Warning signs are put up along roads where there are often winds.

Winds can be strong enough to push a lorry over.

Windsurfers need wind to blow them across the water.

Some winds are useful and some can be used for fun. We can use winds over the sea to sail boats and windsurf.

Disaster: tornado

Tornadoes are one of the most dangerous types of weather. They are also called whirlwinds or twisters because the air inside them spins very fast.

The spinning **funnel** of a tornado stretches down from a storm cloud to the ground.

Tornadoes can lift and
then drop large objects.
They can even
destroy houses.

Many tornadoes only last a few minutes.
In that short time they can travel a
long way. A tornado can destroy
almost anything in its path.

Wind power

Windmills have been using wind power for hundreds of years. The wind pushes the sails round. The sails turn machinery for grinding grain or moving water.

Machinery in this windmill changes grain into flour for making bread.

The energy from these wind turbines is used to work lighting and machinery in towns and cities.

Wind **turbines** use the wind to make energy. They have blades that go round in the wind. The turning of the blades is made into **electricity**.

Project: where is the wind coming from?

Find out the direction of the wind where you live. Firstly, you will need to make a wind sock.

You will need:
- A4 sheet of paper
- scissors
- sticky tape
- tissue paper
- paper clip
- needle and cotton
- compass
- pole

1. Fold the paper over three times to make a strip.

2. Cut the tissue paper into long thin streamers.

3. Tape one end of each streamer to the strip.

4. Tape the ends of the strip together to make a narrow tube, with the streamers coming out of it.

5. Use the needle to push four holes in the tube. Thread cotton through each hole. Tie all the ends of the cotton together.

6. Tie the windsock to a pole with cotton.

7. Use a compass to check the wind direction. Check it a few times during one day to see if it changes.

Ask a grown-up to help you.

Glossary

anemometer instrument used for measuring the speed of the wind

breeze gentle wind

crop plants that are grown to eat or sell

electricity energy that powers machinery and lights

funnel shape of a tornado. A tornado is wide at the top and thin at the bottom

gale fast wind that can do a lot of damage

hurricane storm that brings powerful winds and lots of rain

monsoon summer wind that brings lots of rain

power lines wires that carry electricity to where it is needed

temperature how hot or cold something is

tornado storm with winds that spin very fast

turbine machine with blades that turn very fast to make energy

weather vane instrument that blows round to show the direction of the wind

windbreak barrier that protects plants or people from the wind

Find out more

More books to read

Bright Sparks: Wild, Wet and Windy, Claire Llewellyn (Walker Books, 1997)

A Closer Look at Hurricanes and Typhoons, Jen Green (Franklin Watts, 1996)

What is Weather: Wind, Miranda Ashwell and Andy Owen (Heinemann Library, 2000)

Websites to visit

http://www.bbc.co.uk/weather/weatherwise
A website packed with information about how the weather affects us, weather images and facts, and lots of fun games, projects and activities.

http://www.onlineweather.com
Find out and look at what the weather is like all around the world.

Index

Titles in the *Watching the Weather* series include:

Hardback   0 431 19022 4

Hardback   0 431 19023 2

Hardback   0 431 19024 0

Hardback   0 431 19025 9

Hardback   0 431 19026 7

Hardback   0 431 19035 6

Hardback   0 431 19036 4

Hardback   0 431 19037 2

Hardback   0 431 19034 8

Find out about the other titles in this series on our website www.heinemann.co.uk/library